# WE'RE SOMEWHERE ELSE NOW

Also by Robyn Sarah

POETRY

*Wherever We Mean to Be: Selected Poems 1975-2015* (2017)
*My Shoes Are Killing Me* (2015)
*Digressions: Prose Poems, Collage Poems, and Sketches* (2012)
*Pause for Breath* (2009)
*A Day's Grace* (2003)
*Questions About The Stars* (1998)
*The Touchstone: Poems New and Selected* (1992)
*Becoming Light* (1987)
*Anyone Skating On That Middle Ground* (1984)
*The Space Between Sleep and Waking* (1981)
*Shadowplay* (1978)

SHORT STORIES

*Promise of Shelter* (1997)
*A Nice Gazebo* (1992)

MEMOIR

*Music, Late and Soon* (2021)

CRITICISM

*Little Eurekas: A Decade's Thoughts on Poetry* (2007)

IN TRANSLATION

*Le tamis des jours: Poèmes choisis* (2007)
Translated by Marie Frankland; Préface by Pierre Nepveu

*Mes souliers me font mourir* (2019)
Translated by Rémi Labrecque

ROBYN SARAH

# WE'RE SOMEWHERE ELSE NOW

*Poems 2016–2024*

BIBLIOASIS
WINDSOR, ONTARIO

FIRST EDITION
10 9 8 7 6 5 4 3 2 1

*Library and Archives Canada Cataloguing in Publication*
Title: We're somewhere else now : poems 2016–2024 / Robyn Sarah.
Other titles: We are somewhere else now
Names: Sarah, Robyn, author.
Identifiers: Canadiana (print) 20250238144 | Canadiana (ebook) 20250240432
ISBN 9781771966863 (softcover) | ISBN 9781771966870 (EPUB)
Subjects: LCGFT: Poetry.
Classification: LCC PS8587.A3765 W47 2025 | DDC C811/.54—dc23

Edited by Vanessa Stauffer
Copyedited by Emily Donaldson
Cover designed by Vanessa Stauffer
Cover photograph by César_Tv

Biblioasis acknowledges the support of the Canada Council for the Arts and funding support from the Ontario Arts Council and the Government of Ontario, including through the Ontario Book Publishing Tax Credit and Ontario Creates.

PRINTED AND BOUND IN CANADA

*for my generation*

PART ONE

## ONCE MORE

*(thirty-one poems)*

PART TWO

## IN THE WILDERNESS

*(A Soliloquy, in broken time)*

PART ONE ❧

# ONCE MORE

It is equal to living in a tragic land
To live in a tragic time.
*—Wallace Stevens, "Dry Loaf"*

Rough winds do shake the darling buds of May.
*—William Shakespeare, Sonnet* XVIII

## CHANDELIER

I woke up one day and the world was out there, roaring and being the world, almost as though nothing had happened.

The rest of the interrupted sentence was not gone; it had somehow jumped to the bottom of the screen.

Evidence was mounting that we had been hoodwinked, that we were smoke-and-mirrored. But the room was always exactly as we left it.

An enormous *Why* had begun to form in the sky, and hundreds of smaller why's suddenly materialized, hanging from the tips of bare branches, disguised as raindrops.

It was a kind of chandelier that hung there above our heads – not so very far above our heads. But no one was looking up.

Trees were falling silently in forests all over the world.

## LATE JOURNAL ENTRY ON A LEAP YEAR'S PHANTOM DAY

And how many times can we say
and how many ways can we say
this life's ephemeral?
That the day
is dying even as we list
its beauties to remember
(may none be missed!)
on a fresh page,
under its rare numeral
in the cycle of days?

– Flimsy, too, is paper.

This twenty-ninth is nearly over.
Only the afterglow
of late sun bathes
the pale stone of that convent steeple
seen through distant bare trees.
It is fading as I look.
Soon it will be dark.

This day has leapt.

Not for another four
years will there come
again one of its number.

## FINDERS KEEPERS LOSERS WEEPERS

(twelve miniatures)

### i

The Lost and Found.
Amazing grace, to be reunited
with the sentimental scarf,
pulled like a magician's rabbit
out of the snarl and hotchpotch
of a mildewed wooden crate
fished from beneath the counter.

ii

While buying a potted narcissus
at the Atwater Market
to bring to the hostess at dinner,
she lost a diamond
from her grandmother's ring.
What an expensive flower!

iii

Grownups look up. They look around.
*Tomorrow may be sunny.*
Children live closer to the ground.
They find the money.

iv

Sometimes a brook-pebble, wet and white
with a green blush, or marbled green,
turns out, to a finger's touch,
to be coated thinly in slime,
its verdigris no boon
but an algae bloom.
What seemed a find
has lost what made it one –
barely a moment prized,
then tossed, for the brook to claim.

v

Struck through dark water
by a stray ray of sun:
a fish-lure, gleaming like a jewel
in the silty mud at lake-bottom.
Struck in the eye – luck-struck –
(one in a row of five):
the boy on the dock
who spotted it first, and dived.

vi

The rag-bag's full.
All these bright bits, kept
for a rainy day – but now
the sewing machine
is frozen stiff with rust,
the eye that threads the needle
can't find the needle's eye.

vii

The din of summer insect sound
has thinned
to a single cricket.

viii

We keep a loved animal,
one day to weep its passing.
"Lost Cat" signs fray and fade
through winter, taped to the lampposts.
Night after night a woman walks the alley,
calling, calling, calling – through our sleep
we hear her two-note whistle.
Yet some go unreported: the found cat,
shut for the morning in the music-room,
turns out to match no classifieds,
no hand-taped notice, far or near.
We advertise, get no replies.
She'll find a home here.

ix

Stripped of assets, livelihood, position,
citizenship and papers; forced to abandon
home and everything within; country and kin;
bereaved of loved ones, then relieved
of one's baggage, of the very clothes
off one's back – all of one's substance,
all that was *on one's person*, gone –
this happens to some. Too many have been
reduced to "their person." The human unit.
*Poor, bare, forked animal.*
When nothing's left to take away,
is there some gain?

x

The more we lose,
the closer we come
to who we are.

xi

There are words we keep.
Words on paper: clippings,
quotations, letters. Words in our heads,
words that we "have by heart":
poems, proverbs, prayers.
There are words that keep us.
Do we keep our word?

xii

For a few moments
the cushion still keeps
the warmth of the cat
that slept there all morning.

~

## PLANTINGS

Hope breaks ground undiminished
   from bulbs of buried sorrow,
as leaving things unfinished
   gives purpose to the morrow.

## LIT ROOM

> Do not read 'your children' [*banayikh*] but 'your builders' [*bonayikh*].
>
> – Talmud, Berakhot 64A

In a morning kitchen, a child begins his day. Tilting his head from side to side and bouncing a little on his heels – he's singing. You can't hear him, you are seeing him in the frame of a facing window – lit room to lit room – across a narrow courtyard on a winter dawn. Enter his parents, singly, one just after the other. In the middle of the kitchen they pause to embrace, to kiss good morning. The small boy in pajamas scooped up in his father's arms and lifted to the window for a moment. Now set down again, in his furry pajamas with feet. And he's off –

Above their third-floor window, along the roof's edge, starlings huddle in a row. Winter bird-breath comes in little puffs of lit-up steam. Small icicles like teeth hang from the flashing. From the chimney, smoke flies in ribbons, tinged pink as the newly risen sun crests the roofline.

The little child-head floats about the room, just above the level of the window-sill. Erratic movements of a child. Zig-zag. Zig and zag. (What governs the zigs and zags? Who can ever know?) The child is busy being a child. A busy being, a child. The mother is busy, too – she's at the stove now, stirring something in a pot. Making breakfast. You know it's nothing special, it is just breakfast. An everyday feast.

Feast of the everyday. A man and a woman and a child in a third-floor kitchen, framed in a lit window. What architecture! Their building soars heavenwards.

## IN THE MEDICAL BUILDING LOBBY CAFÉ

She is looking at him
out of her old face
with her young eyes.
Eyes that still appreciate
a tall young man with a nice face,
a strong frame, a young man's
loose-limbed, purposeful stride –
*this* young man, striding her way.
When she looks out of her
young eyes, she forgets her face
is no longer young, she forgets
her face. She expects – *what*
does she expect? – her glance
to be met, that's all. That flash
connection in passing, split-
second signal exchanged between
strangers, fellow humans –
subliminal salutation –
no more than that!
                                        But he,
easy of motion, at ease in his skin,
glides on by. Registers her look
a bit absently; files it as requiring
no response. His eyes don't even
seem to know they've done that.
(His eyes, that saw only
an old face.
                    Hers.)

## PERPETUAL

I woke with the word PERPETUAL in my head, and for a few moments I thought there was something I could do with it. But there wasn't. Whatever was shiny about it went dull before I could fully open my eyes, and when I put out a finger to see if I could dust it off, it shattered like a Christmas tree bauble. I woke with the word SMITHEREENS in my head.

It was the same old world I woke to.

It was the same old world forever changing,
the way a soft brown moth seems to melt into air
when you try to clap it between your hands,

the way we stoop on the autumn street to pick up
one fallen leaf exceptional in its colours,
and walk some little way admiring it
before letting it drop again.

## FOUND POEM, WITH CODA

(from *Latin for Today: Book One.*)

You have learned that the endings
of Latin nouns and verbs
are important. *The study of Latin*
*is very largely the study of endings.*

( – So, too, the study of Rome.)

## A FESTERING

On the site of an old
injury, buried deep
under the closed skin

an itch begins,
an itch
the scratch of which

may yield a poem
or a theorem, or unearth
the seed of a great invention

that will unseat
all our assumptions
and rewind Time.

A small insistent itch
under a patch of newer skin
that doesn't match –

something inside that wants
to birth, or hatch,
work its way out

from under a healing
that was incomplete.
So it can all begin

again, from scratch.

## LE RAPPEL DES OISEAUX

Call the birds back.
 The one of the bent wings, call him back,
 and the dark one that fell without a sound,
 and the white one that rose from the water.
Call back the coloured ones that sang in the wine,
Call back the coloured ones that glittered in the dream.
Call the birds back, one by one.
Call them by their secret names.

 The one of the bent wings fell spiralling,
 the dark one came down like a cinder,
 the white one beat against the air.
The coloured ones drifted to the bottom of the glass
like leaves in a still, small pool.

Call the birds back, one by one.
 They flew up from the green meadow,
 they mounted to the sun,
 they tempted the wings of the whirlwind,
 they descended into the chasm.
  There, in near dark,
  their sad voices
  answer each other.

They trouble the ears of the wakeful.
They steal men's wits.
By the light of day they were glorious.
They have fallen past falling.

O call them back!

Call the birds back, one by one,
Call them by their secret names.

For months now, how many months – I've lost count – I wake to ghost birds. A soundscape of birds at dawn, but heard from far, far away. It doesn't happen every day. I only hear it if I wake just before dawn. It's something my mind imposes on the silence, or extrapolates from the faint ambient sounds of the house – hum of the air cleaner, gurgling in the pipes. It's a memory of birdsong at dawn that we no longer hear in this neighbourhood. It's my mind trying to bring the birds back.

When it began, the soundscapes were so true to life that wishful thinking sometimes impelled me to jump out of bed and open the window, on the chance this wasn't just a waking dream or a shifting of fluid in my inner ear. But opening the window only confirmed what I already knew: it was silent out there. It was still dark. The sounds were in my head.

My ghost birds. I can hear the near and far of them, the layers of birdsong, nearer birds and farther birds, foreground and background. And strangely, it's as if they're contained in a frame – it's a tableau, a tapestry – as if I can visualize the sounds I'm hearing, some at the edges of the frame, some nearer the middle, in clusters or overlapping, criss-crossing, an embroidery of sound. All the different kinds of chirp – the birds that cheep and chirrup, the birds that whistle and warble, some loud and glittering, others subdued or muted by distance. The complex textures of their interaction, a counterpoint so familiar – playback of a soundtrack my mind must have recorded long ago without my knowing it, or how could I hear them now in such detail?

Did I know I had all of these songs saved in my head, once it registered that we had stopped hearing them in real life?

Did I ever really hear them, before memory gave them back?

## SHADOWS IN SPRINGTIME

*May, 2020 (for Roman Wolfe)*

Little boy, grandchild I waited
so long for,
                    play with me.
Play
            six feet away,         six feet
too far away                I with the sun
behind my shoulder,
                              you
on a sidewalk square
lit by the sun in May –

sun that has given me
shadow-arms, extending
the reach of my living arms
that may not touch you, hold you,
my empty arms in Virus Time –

but with my living hands, see!
I can make shadow-hands, reaching
all the way to where you sit, I can make
animal shadows on the sidewalk
for you to chase and grab at,
laughing – so we play,
we play in Virus Time.

Little boy sitting on a sidewalk square
lit by May sunshine          six feet far,
          six feet too far away,
still we can play, and I can touch you
with my shadow hands

You who can't yet walk alone
(though you can *dance to your daddy,*
                    *my little laddie*
holding his hands, grandson and son)

– little one, let me dance
a circle round the two of you
with six-foot radius

*dance-dance*

tracing a wheel around you, face to face –
your faces at the centre turning
to follow mine,
always six feet between

and let me stomp a rhythm
to make you laugh,
to hear your laugh,
its sweet chime
in Virus Time

*dance-dance*

six feet (our own)
stomping the rhythm together now,
double arm's length apart
too far,
real arm and shadow arm
a six-foot span

*dance-dance*

but there you are,

so almost-near,

*and I can touch you with my shadow hands*

## DO-SI-DO

Four sparrows jockey for a perch
on a four-perch hanging feeder,
then
        flutter and jostle, each
to unseat another for a better,

           switching rungs
                again
                   and then
            again

their feathered exchange
a square-dance maneuver
with chitter for patter:
four-flit criss-cross
on a two-step ladder.

## THE LAST GOOD DAYS

I wanted to write a book called
*The Last Good Days on Earth*
this was some while back, when I thought
we were living them, but maybe
we're living them now, even though
I hardly remember how things were
when I last thought the days were
good, maybe the days are still good
maybe less and less becomes more
and more as we cling to what's left
(mainly our belief that we haven't lost
all that much, or that anyway "this will pass"
and "things have to get better soon")

but I remember other times on the balcony
in the last of sunset glow, or snug in bed
hearing sudden hard rain or night wind
filling a big tree (things we still have
that are somehow not what they were)
– I remember when life was still
an open book to write in,
many pages still clean.

## AN ABDICATION

Anonymous as a twenty dollar bill
blowing down the street, tumbling
over and over along the pavement
in a gusting wind

he was well on his way to becoming
a nobody – he who had never been
anybody much to begin with.
He was becoming a zhivago,

becoming like Zhivago after the suicide
of Strelnikov: the doctor gone to seed,
forgetting his skills at doctoring,
his knowledge, his passion for writing,

arriving in the city in rags and foot cloths,
having sold the clothes off his back for food.
There are different ways of becoming
a zhivago. This one begins with a poet's

not much caring whether he ever
publishes another word; progresses
to not much caring whether he
ever writes one; and thence

to not answering emails,
to not reading them,
and finally to a moment of truth
one sultry summer afternoon

as he finds himself killing flies
with an old paperback copy
of John Ashbery's
*Houseboat Days*.

## IN LOCKDOWN

(Montreal, 2021)

On a lamp post at the corner of Parc
and Villeneuve, someone has printed
in permanent black marker
NO HAPPINESS EVER.
A block away, on the alley,
on the side of a concrete foundation
someone else has painted in white cursive
*Jusqu'à ce que l'amour nous sépare*

despair in two languages

I imagine the days of the unhappy kid
a boy, I think, mid-teens, cut off
from friends, sports
from just hanging out
in the places kids hang out
corner pool-hall, pizza joint
familiar haunts all closed

and days of the woman
put to the test of "two's company"
(two shut in together
with no end in sight)
who for love's sake forced an end
and asked her partner to move out

## BALLAD OF THE ONE YEAR BRIDE

Mother, the days are sweet
and the garden grows.
Outside our bedroom window
the green elm blows.

Mother, the days are good
at the season's turning.
The elm lets fall its leaves
and we watch them burning.

Mother, the days are short.
Wind seeps through cracks.
The elm is chalked with snow
and the birds leave tracks.

Oh mother, the snow is gone
and the spring comes surely.
No leaves are upon the elm
that was blighted early.

And I put by my letters,
and no more write.
Outside our bedroom window
elm bones turn white.

## REPRISE

A sound from childhood, suddenly recalled:
the music of a pet bird's beak and claws
as it clambers up and down
the sides of its cage,
like random harp strings being plucked –

A mellow metallic music played
upon the bars, a ringing, as it climbs
up, down and all around
and over the ceiling upside down,
cocking a bright eye upward,

                    or – if the door
                    hangs open on its hinge –
                    venturing out, to climb
                    all over the outside of the cage
                    and up to the vaulted roof,
                    cocking the same eye down and in,
                    then up, and all about,
                    ready to take wing.

By what trick of the mind
does it now seem, in memory,
the music played from without
had a sweeter ring?

## FLASHBACK (MARCH 21, 2020)

We're afraid to ask. A woman employee in the pharmacy took me to the back of the store and pointed to a bin that looked empty, but in the bottom there was one last bottle. Was she saving it for someone? Every week feels like a month; most days, most of the day, paralyzed by indecision. Still it was good to have an excuse to walk outside into a spring rain …

Water-drops hanging from the balcony rail as a hedge against bank collapse. A fist fight over lettuce, witnessed in the grocery store. The streets quiet. Buses rolling by nearly empty. Everyone downtown was wearing masks; uptown they were carrying jumbo packs of toilet paper. A welcome sighting of Quasimodo, through plate glass, mopping the floor of the closed and empty restaurant.

There was a black ribbon across the entrance to the bank. The impervious clerk who mans the central desk stood by the door, letting people in one or two at a time. He explained, "It's because of the wires." "The wires? What wires?" "It's because of the wirus." (Oh, the *wirus.*) More black ribbons inside. "Stand behind the ribbon." The teller was wearing blue latex gloves. Now it all makes sense. But does it?

Back home the balcony was cluttered with end-of-winter mess, but there was room for two chairs. Alternating between fury and hilarity, we sat. Some diluted sun, last sun of the day, broke through cloud cover. Old dirty snow at our feet; spilled dirt from plant pots, spilled seed from the dollar-store bird feeder bought on impulse just before the marching orders came down: *March in place.* The sparrows come every day and are no longer afraid. All of them now wearing gloves.

## STRAWS

Everyone looking through their straw.
And maybe it's best that way,

a collective shield, silent pact
to protect self and others by continuing
to pursue one's own business as usual,
as if it were all just business as usual,
colluding to ignore that giant shadow
in the peripheral vision, as it creeps
ever closer to where we stand

you could call it high flying denial
or you could call it kindness,
kindness or willful blindness –
hearts in the right place
or heads in the sand

Headline: *Great Disorder*
*in the Next Eighteen Months.*
Well, wait a minute. Who says?
Who has the authority to proclaim?
And besides – *who doesn't know that?*

We know it and we don't.

Hearts in the right place
won't be enough to save us.
We need accidents.

## STREET HOCKEY ON HUTCHISON AND VILLENEUVE, 1981

*November. The after-school games*
*on the corner have gotten shorter,*
*dark now at five,*
*and waves of dry leaves*
*blowing along the ground*
*as streetlamps flicker to life*

You close your eyes and see them again,
the players, forty years ago on this block,
nameless boys (your own, your firstborn,
now himself a parent, then still too young
for street play, intent on toy boats in his bath
while supper simmered on the stove)
– again you seem to hear the slap
of sticks on pavement, sometimes a shout,
muted by windows lately shut
against the cold, and you recall
a melancholy cast to the scene out there,
the boys in their dark jackets, the daylight
fading quickly, and the ghostly effect
of those leaves blowing down the street,
dry-brown, wasted, aimless,
crossing the path of the game.

## NOTHING'S HAPPENING HERE

Nothing's happening here, I thought,
crumpling a page of early-morning scrawl.
But then I switched off the electric heater
and silence happened.

Layers of cloud are sailing past the high-rise
seen from the lane-side window – balconies
stacked skyward like open bureau drawers
spilling out glimpses of messy lives.

A wind in the backyard tree
shakes the winter-stiff twigs,
a squirrel in the fork
washes his face with both hands.

Hope for the world these days
I hardly dare, but flowers joy me,
last night's bouquet
sunstruck on the breakfast table.

The great mill of the press keeps spinning its
fine twisted linen, turning dirty laundry
into emperor's clothes

and the spider in the window also spins,
absorbed in its thread of purpose
between inner and outer panes.

## ON READING HOPKINS' *NO WORST, THERE IS NONE . . .*

A single soul's relief, and not for long,
Is the cry of grief, out of the belly torn.
But solace for generations yet unborn
Is the grief-cry channeled into poem or song.

## ONCE MORE

**1**

Friends have passed on – too soon, and suddenly.
Two in as many months. With each, we had
Scant time to catch our breath between the sad
Verdict first shared, and sad finality.
The years of making memories are gone.
We did not know those years for what they were.
All seems in flux. Dark forces are astir.
Children have grown and flown. Friends have passed on.

We dreamed a world untouched by war or want.
We lived a lie that we believed and preached.
Now we can't look the future in the eye.
As spring arrives once more, with airs that haunt,
We turn, gaze backward where our hopes lie beached.
Old men come out to watch the world go by.

**2**

Old men (come out to watch the world go by,
As old men ever will) know what they know.
They weren't born yesterday. New winds that blow
To them are winds remembered, winds that lie.
Stalwart, they stand like pillars in the sun,
Or lean on porch rails, testing with their weight
Another winter's wobble to set straight,
A seasonal adjustment to be done.

Old men in springtime don't look far ahead.
This April's crocuses have broken ground.
Next April's crocuses – well, who can say?
Their garden tools lie rusting in the shed.
They nod to neighbours as they gaze around.
They sun themselves. Let someone else make hay.

**3**

They sun themselves; let someone else make hay.
Their houses have grown old with them. They choose
Their battles wisely, know the ones they'd lose;
The porch rail can be fixed in just a day.
Weeks on, the young in one another's arms
Sweetly entangled, lie on the greening grass
Oblivious to the eyes of all who pass,
Steeped in the moment, lost in each other's charms.

The young in springtime don't look far ahead.
Their time is timeless, every day a world.
An all-consuming "Now" holds them in thrall;
No mighty strivings yet, no nameless dread.
Unguessed, their futures wait, still tightly furled.
Summer unborn, who can imagine fall?

## 4

Summer unborn, who gives a thought to fall?
Summer will overtake them, just the same,
Wrestle them down and bind them to a frame,
The baby carriage in the entrance hall.
Tethers of silk will hold them twenty years.
Moments that stun will bring them to their knees.
They in their turn, makers of memories,
Will float brave hopes and fend off dogging fears.

We turn, gaze back to where our own brave hopes
Foundered and ran aground to lodge in sand.
Under what colours did we first set sail?
We had a map. We thought we knew the ropes.
*We* were the future. All would go as planned.
(We learned the many ways a plan can fail.)

## 5

We learned the ins and outs of plans that fail.
We had our shot at family, work, and love,
And fame, and fortune, and our chance to prove
Some noble dream wherein we could prevail
In service of a greater good. We tried.
We learned to temper expectations, own
Our modest winnings, rather than bemoan
False starts, wrong turns, and gambits fallen wide.

In short, we did what humans do. We rode
The winds of our own times, for good or ill –
Sometimes they favoured human enterprise,
Sometimes they hindered it. The winds have slowed,
Or is it we ourselves – who now stand still,
A hush around our ears, as motion dies?

**6**

The hush around our ears as motion dies
Dismays.  We dreamed a world untouched by war,
Yet war and want rage on – a distant roar.
On air, new journalists repeat old lies
We once believed, or half-believed.  Now doubt
Has taken over; things we thought were true
Hang in the balance, things we thought we knew.
It isn't something you can talk about.

All seems in flux, unhinged, a world gone strange.
Do we imagine this, or is it real?
Children have grown and flown – their visits brief,
They and their young ones headed into change
Beyond imagining.  How will they deal?
Don't ask.  A robin sings.  Trees are in leaf.

## 7

Outside, a robin sings. Trees are in leaf,
Their green lace tossing in the wind. A friend
From far away has just arrived to spend
A day or two in fellowship of grief
For one we loved in common – laid to rest –
With whom we shared some long-ago green hours.
(Before the world wide web, before the towers.
When years for making memories seemed blessed.)

Dark forces are astir, but air of spring
Wafts lilac through the screen once more. For now,
A voice, a face – familiar company;
A word, a touch of hand; remembering.
Friends have passed on – too soon, and suddenly.
We will go on from here. Don't ask us how.

## WORLD AWAITING WAR

spring will soon
slip
forgotten into the cave spaces
beneath rocks

let us remember the time of our coming

for April rustled away like tinsel
and the late leaves were born without voices

The light spurts off the pavement's broken glass.

breathe lilac and look at stars
sway to the twisted
eloquence of apple trees
blow
the snow from dandelions
for it will not rain again

dazed in a dry season
let us remember the time of our coming
before May too
slides like a snake into the crack in the rock

it will not rain again
bells across the evening
will call
will call us to the last burning

## ANOTHER WINTER

Winter is here once more.
(What were we expecting?)
Winter has crept up on us.

The leaves came down on schedule
when we weren't watching
(weren't watching the leaves, that is) –
we were watching the news
instead of the leaves,
and one day we woke
to bare trees and frozen puddles,
wondering how we missed the colours.

As for summer – *was* there a summer?
Why don't we remember?

Look outside:
it's a day without brine,
sky bland as the white
of a hardboiled egg,
no flakes in the air today,
no frost-ferns on the window,
gaiety in abeyance

only another winter day,
only the cold, and the early dark,
and a growing desire to mend fences

maybe a wish or two, quiet ones:
to get a few things done
while we still can,
a few things, slowly,
one by one,

and to see, and to see, and to see

## FOUR CUT SUNFLOWERS, ONE UPSIDE DOWN

That the cut sunflower, spent and drying,
is as wonderful as the sunflower in its striving,

as the sunflower shouting glory from a yellow vase
with thirteen others of its kind,

is something it takes a Van Gogh
to show us. The four cut flowers, tumbled,
lying prone with stems upcurled,
heads disheveled, one overlapping the next,
the fourth face-down – petals now shrunk
to yellow stubs, yet still like wayward flames
forming a shag of crown around the dense
beadwork of centres,

this third and twisted flowering
a last dance on the way
to somewhere else

And from the painter's letters, these lines:

"*When a rough man bears blossoms*
*like a flowering plant*, yes, that is
beautiful to see; but before that *he*

has had to stand a great deal
of winter cold, more than those
who later sympathize with him know."

## LIKE SHADOWS ON GLASS

Let us reinvent love, in this room
from which so much liveliness has fled.
Let's burn some old chairs to keep warm.

Let's reinvent the wheel in this room,
saving a chair-rung for a spindle.
Let's tell each other yarns.

One wakes up and tries
to live well by one's own lights
for one more day

living our lives
(living our lies)
like shadows on glass,

guessing at where our human footprints
disappear on the map
of future time.

No one understood the music
until the music stopped,
and then only a few understood.

## ON READING HOPKINS' *MY OWN HEART LET ME MORE HAVE PITY ON . . .*

In a dark vale, a lovely mile lit
By a long-dead poet – the forms, forms unforeseen
God's smile can take ! As – see ! a sonnet's sheen
Come upon by surprise – words deftly knit
To send out rays of light, like the swift flit
And swoop a goldfinch makes across the green :
Lines on a page, that flash in the in-between
Of darksome hours, releasing truth and wit . . .

– Releasing *self*, from self-obsessing maze !
How does one tender thanks for such a gift ?
For the untangling of what frays and flays
The captive spirit : this unhoped-for shift
Of mind – *crooked made straight !* – how, but to praise
God, in the God-sent words that sparked this lift ?

## INVOCATION

Hope – like a dormant fly
that suddenly revives and begins to buzz
in a corner of the window-screen

Hope – like the mailman's footsteps
coming up the outdoor staircase

Hope – like a paper flower bought
for a handful of loose change
from the woman on the corner by the bank
with her soft Irish lilt (hope like that lilt,
and her hands that made the flower)

Hope – like tiny rainbows cast on the wall
by a crystal hung in a sunny window,
and like the cat that leaps to bat at them
with a velvet paw

Hope – like a sentence underscored
in a borrowed book, or a note in the margin
by a sidelined paragraph, saying: *This is me*

Hope like a shift in the wind,
like a tug on the line,
like a line thrown just in time

Hope – like a phrase heard in a dream
and remembered on waking,
like a floating night-thought
remembered on waking,

remembered again, a few hours later,
and again at evening – a good thought

Hope, come back to me.

## ENVOI

(Artist's Statement)

I do not speak
for the voiceless masses, no.
Nor for the poor, for women, or
for Canada, the True North Strong and Free.
Nor for my other Country 'Tis of Thee.
Not for "my people" (whoever they may be),
nor yet for poets or for poetry.

I do not presume
to speak for anyone but me,
but hope that speaks for Us.

I "speak." That is to say –
I say what I see, and suss
what I must think is true
from seeing what I say.

It might boil down to *I was here.*

Put differently:
I leave my bird-tracks
in fresh-fallen snow,
and fly away.

## PART TWO ∾

# IN THE WILDERNESS

*A Soliloquy, in broken time*

Let the cleansing boom
be thunder,
And let the rain
be rain.

*Sum, ergo dubito.*

## ~ I LAST CALL

1

*Scroll backward to Before, if you can find the spot.*
*Play back the last ride home with unmasked faces:*

Hawks hang in the blue. The tops
of mountainous cumulus lying low
towards the horizon are lit by sun,
yellowing sun of late afternoon
lighting the landscape that flies
past train windows, lighting a scrap yard's
mash of metal – gleam of mashed cars
and car parts, jumble of colours
in a huge heap in a huge pit dug
into the yellow dun of dry spring ground.
The trees still bare, but for the
weeping willows here and there,
the willow branches fringed
in tiny gold, the yellow willows'
windy tresses tossing in the stir
of sun-warmed air . . .

Doubt can kill faith. But it can also
give birth to it. A paradox.

The woman who wheels a cart of snacks
past your coach seat – Does she doubt?
Her voice, her laugh –
strong and deep as the lines
cut around her smile – these are
things you can believe in.
She is of an age, but carries it
with grace. You can see
life still holds out a few bouquets
she thinks it will toss her way.

Last call for snacks and drinks . . .

– Later, the toddler, dumbstruck
by who knows what,
who totters suddenly and sits
down smack
on a hot air grate on the pavement
outside the subway station –
does he doubt?  He looks around
to see who's seen, so he can know
whether to laugh or cry as he scrambles
up again.  We can believe in him.

*Back to the sea!* shouted the brave puppet.

(Man, tatterdemalion man,
let me stand close to your fire.)

2

It began in winter.
It began
as winter was beginning –

the year's first snowflakes were dancing
with the year's last yellow leaves
in an early morning wind.

The cat was making silk.
That's what cats do when they sleep.
The cat was making silk out of sleep

when a voice inside me
spoke suddenly, saying
*I am, therefore I doubt.*

3

Trouble in your life
doesn't always arrive announced.
It need not burst upon you
like a blowing of horns.
Sometimes it creeps up unwatched.
In the middle of the night a noise
you can't do anything about:
plaster falling inside the walls
in little showers,
old plaster, cracked and crumbling,
dislodged by slow contraction
and winter dryness,
or nudged by mice –
an old house falling apart
in its innards,
invisibly.

Tremble in your life

*Tremble and do not sin; commune with your own heart upon your bed, and be still.*

4

Cracks and pops of an old house
in winter.  And the low hum
of the heating system
like a ship's engine,
how it carries us
over the winter waves.

Things people don't understand:
Civil war doesn't announce itself.
There isn't a declaration.
There isn't a day when it begins.
And that cleansing boom
we think might set things straight
might not do that.
Might not even come.

The smartly dressed woman at the podium
has come a long way to tell us
what we must think and do.
She seems to know.
"Are there any questions?"
(Oh, lady.  There are nothing but.)

Doubt does not take the form
of questions voiced politely from the floor.
Doubt comes up from the silent howl
at the centre of us,
like a voice from the vortex
beneath plates that shift and rub,
the earth's fontanelle –
up from down deep, it comes.

*I don't know.*  Say it.
Three wonderful, counterintuitive words.
Terrifying words.

**5**

Time, in the days before screens.
On the wall each month, a new
grid of numbered squares
soon to crowd up with scrawl
in a crabbed hand:
*Do this. Get that.*
*Be in this place, at that hour.*
Tearing off the pages one by one . . .

Why put a name on a day?
How can it matter what a day is called?
The cat doesn't know it's Tuesday.
Human purpose tracks our hours.

Time like an oil – sliding
Time like a jelly – encasing
Time like a muscle – flexing

How can the sun slip
so far aslant, so swiftly?

The cheeping of sparrows heard
through winter-sealed windows
comes as a straw of cheer
on the year's shortest day.

The seed inside its pod
waits out the season.

6

I am; therefore I doubt.
(*Am I? Do I?*)

To be. To do.
To be a doer.
To be a door.
*Knock, knock. Who's there?*

How far back would we have to turn the clock
to be able to be happy in the old ways?

We were a generation in the woods.
We were not raised in faith, but God
was still the backbone of the world we knew;
we paid lip service to that standing frame.
God was the backbone though we didn't know it.
If God was dead, we were his obit.

How will we talk to godless grandchildren?

7

I was beginning to see Doubt as a character. A fiddler. Maybe androgynous. Doubt as a tall, lean, androgynous fiddler.

*In the beginning God created the heaven and the earth* – then there was doubt. Then there was a new kind of certainty that called itself Enlightenment. But soon enough, a thin sound of fiddling could be heard out behind the woodshed and Doubt was back. Personified. Asking impertinent questions. *Who says so?*

Do we live our whole lives on hearsay?
Whose hearsay is the truth, and whose is heresy?
Is there a Between?

8

Doubt is a prince today. Dressed as one.
Doubt is a jester. Dressed as one.

And these my thoughts.
(If a cat. If a morning cat
wants its ears rubbed – )

"*Is. Is. Is. Is. Is.*"
"That's what I heard yesterday in the pub."
– The voice of an old friend, in memory.
A voice from the seventies: his imitation
of a stoned-out, mind-blown poet
in a pub at the edge of a wood.
One come stumbling
out of the wood, into the pub.
Crazed-eyed, standing on a table,
raving his IS-ness.

BE HERE NOW was the watchword
of the day. Some of us noticed
it could invert to BE NOWHERE.

– Out of the corner of my eye
a movement. Something glides by, glides
back and forth, insistent. (If a cat.
If a morning cat wants breakfast – )

IS.
Out of nowhere, the word.
Out of the nowhere wood.

9

Someone handed me a word, like a coin. Dull metal, the stamped relief worn almost flat. (Whose head this is I think I know. I learned it in a classroom though. Head of a queen. Still Queen, till queendom gone.)

We crown a head to stamp upon a coin.
We manufacture certainties because we cannot bear
to live unknowing. Living, we hold to certainties
in currency. *Homo Sapiens.* But *do we know?*

> "*Well, what do you know!*" – an expression of what? surprise!
> On finding out something we *didn't* know!

> "*As we all know . . .*" – an expression of what?
> Self-complacency! Other-persuasion!

Can we know what *is* ?
What can we really know beyond a doubt?

Not as much as we think. Not much. Maybe nothing. But if we say "I know nothing," is that not "knowing"? Is it not, perhaps, the profoundest knowing – to be able to say that, as we continue to operate on handed-down certainties?

We operate. Are operatives. Of whom?

## 10

I was at the beginning of something. (Doubt was standing on a rock, in the sunrise, fiddling a new tune. Dressed in the colours of a jester.)

The beginning of cognizance
of some evil at work behind the scenes,
working and lurking
beyond the puppet heads of politicians,
the puppet theatre of a screen
where people park their thinking –
and the screens – everywhere the screens –
what is behind them, what are they screening?

Doubt was the Prince of Nonsense.
(We need the meaningless to give a thing meaning.)

Begin from a beginning:
*I think, therefore I am.*
Do I know what I think?
Do I know what *I* think?
But I know what I know. That is to say,
I believe what I'm told by the ones I'm told
must know. (Can I *know* that they know?)

It has come to pass that I doubt *everything*
and it comes to nothing. Jingle of little bells
on a jester's cap as he shakes his head
up and down – side to side – tilt left, tilt right
signifying *Yes – No – Maybe*

*Signifying nothing* (Macbeth said it)

*Nothing can come of nothing* (Lear said it)

And Tom's a-cold . . .

– Nothing can come of nothing, but *something* can also come of nothing, Macbeth and Lear and all of Shakespeare's host, real to us as people in the flesh . . . we are makers of things, not just shoes and ships and sealing-wax, but songs and symphonies, theorems and theories, ideas . . . things of the mind . . . it is what raises us above the animals

(– ah, but to the sometime peril of the animals,
ourselves included.)

And if Doubt is a fiddler, who am I?

Can I be the accompanist?
Can I accompany the fiddler?

Can I keep company with Doubt
and play the descant?

This is my jam session with Doubt

11

Makers of things, we leave
our marks on the world. Our traces.
Roamers, we happen on marks
of some who came before us.
Thinkers, we ponder these,
read them, read into them.
Hobo marks on the side of a house,
traces we read, traces we leave.
*Here we received*
*sustenance. Bread.*
"This is a good house."

Stone and papyrus hobo marks
marks on parchment
marks on vellum
*(Man does not live by bread alone.)*
"This is a good house."

Hoboes were here.

*We're all freeloaders under God*

12

Famous first words: *Let there be light.*
First words of the One who will have no
last words, being eternal –
or who will endure in silence ever after,
once they have been spoken.

*From everlasting thou art God,*
*To endless years the same.*

(The faith cord came unplugged.
When did that happen? Is there a way
to plug ourselves back in to The Eternal?)

*Everlasting. Eternal.* Words I never thought about. But now they stupefy me. *Infinity. Infinite.* I never thought about those either – or not past childhood, when I first encountered them. Not till just recently, when one morning on the balcony, watching people pass on the street below, it struck me anew – or maybe for the first time – that when we walk outside, there is nothing between the top of our heads and infinite space.

The thought was staggering. That we walk on this planet like ants! (Of course, so do ants.) But we think ourselves so big! I had never appreciated our smallness. Had never considered how we *think* ourselves into bigness. How much bigger are we than ants, really, when we measure that difference against infinite space?

Outer space, inner space – where does the "out" begin? Is inner space also infinite? Are the two contiguous? Can we go so far into ourselves that we invert and find ourselves in outer space? Is one a metaphor for the other?

And where in all this is The Eternal to be found?

13

In the darkness of pre-dawn, Doubt waxes towards being. Mine the only lit window.

Bare branches begin to sway a little in the wind, as if a breath stirred them. As if to say "Wake up." As the spirit of God moved upon the face of the waters.

The air in the cold room was stirring,
warm air pushing cold air.
The heater hummed and my watch
lay on my desk telling the time.
Outside it was not yet light.
The curved stairways ran up and down
in the dark like scales.

Doubt was in the sway of bare branches in the wind, in the inkbottle blue of pre-dawn. And I was in the sway of doubt.

14

Maybe it was an illusion, the new period of certainty. Certainty broke up into certainties and the certainties bounced off each other until they broke into particles and the particles were waves and the waves were a cloud and the cloud was Doubt.

Today Doubt is a cloud, and the cloud is a pillar that ascends into Infinite Space

*– and as I wrote that, the lights went out in my study and my little heater shut off.*

Power failure? or just a blown fuse.

15

Begin from a beginning:

If the spirit of God moved upon the face of the waters, the waters must have been there before God began to speak, before "Let there be light" was spoken. *In the beginning God created the heaven and the earth.* How was this accomplished? Did God say (silently) "Let there be heaven and earth"? *And the earth was without form and void.* But there were waters, and there was "the deep" – there was *darkness upon the face of the deep* before God said "Let there be light" and saw that it was good, and divided it from the darkness, calling the one "day" and the other "night." So ends Day One. Then how account for the firmament God made on the second day, to divide the waters from the waters? *And God called the firmament Heaven* – but wasn't heaven already there? Or was it not fully created until it had been named?

*Why am I thinking about this?*

Why in heaven?
Why on earth.

16

A civilization lost its faith in the old stories. Then it lost even the stories. And with the stories it lost the questions that arise from the stories, and with the questions it lost its foothold in Time, it lost its place, its knowing. The heart of its knowing, which was its very heart.

Know your place.

*Know before Whom you stand.*

*Ha-Makom*, the Place. One of the names of God,
who is not to be found in a place. Who IS the place.

(Doubt was at the edge of the field at the end of the day.
Foraging.)

17

Dead-empty but still coasting, we glide
into a future we never imagined.
Entering into the darkest of days.
We have felt this coming.
We did not know the shape of it.
But we knew its cold breath.
WAS. WAS. WAS. WAS. WAS.

It was the winter of our Disconnect.
It was the end of comfort.
The sun gone from room after room.
Life in the lanes, life on the stoops
already fading in memory.
All eyes on the little screens.

Words in my waking head. Jagged fragments.
Piecemeal. Betweentimes.
Capricious clock. (Did I forget to set it?)
Waiting for clock-crow.
Peace/miel, honey of peace.
(Where is peace? What is the Between?)

In the mirror I saw Doubt, wearing my face. I had become Doubt, embodied.

And the Between hovered in the twilight at the edge of the field. The Between was a rabbit at the edge of the field, a rabbit suddenly darting out into the road, a rabbit caught in the headlights.

18

Once I had some ideas, some positions, some opinions. Now I have Doubt, like a blackbird whistling on my shoulder.

Once, a holy man, witness to vows, told us to guard our Between.

Once, a crazy man, a maker of beautiful things, told us to trust in the Unknown.

I knew a man who came at things sideways, who never answered questions. His silence opened doors in my head.

I had a friend whose last words were *Don't stop the music.*

There are people who fill their homes with Beautiful Things from All Over the World.

And someone is always making noise.

Norm took a slow boat to Rome.

## 19

The way a woman loves the first cat
after the children leave home.
The way a lonely teenage boy loves the dog
that sleeps on the end of his bed.
The way a man and woman love at mid-life
who both are married to others.
With just such an ache do we love our human lives . . .

People happen to each other,
or they don't.  Sometimes they unhappen.
so-called friends      would-be lovers      have-been spouses
the star-crossed ones      *all the lonely people*

It is a door opening on air
where a balcony once was.
It is a door free-standing in a garden,
and Doubt is on the other side of the door.  Not knocking.

> *When he, whose vocation was Waiting, sat far from home –*
> who in his scattered hotel room, shunning the mirror, heard
> how again, in the air, they conferred over his probed heart
> *and passed their judgment:  that it did not have love . . .*

(As the drop of a star
from nowhere into nowhere
burns its arc across the eyeball
but leaves the sky unscarred,
so fly our pinprick lives,
their arc across the Eye
of the Knowing One.
And some arcs intersect.  Yet two
who look into each other's eyes
and cannot look away,
they also cannot say
what they see there.)

20

When the eyes begin to fail. When the edges of things begin to blur. When eyesight becomes vision. Isn't "eyesight" a redundancy? But it implies another kind of sight. If edges are lost, all blends into a oneness and is that not what visionaries say existence really is?

We open our eyes at birth to the oneness, but when we begin to see, what we see is separation. We learn the world by separating things we see. Learning their thingness: by shape, by colour, by motion, by function, by purpose. Learning their usefulness to us, our agency over them. Learning the names they have been given.

*And the earth was without form and void.*
Then separation began.

And dominion.
*(The world is so full of a number of things,*
*I think we should all be as happy as kings,*
wrote a rhymester for children.)

But what of those things? Rilke's Things – the Tao's Ten Thousand Things – *No ideas but in things* ? How shall we know them?

> *Work of the eyes is done, now*
> *go and do heart-work*

## 21

In the middle of January, the sun.
Like a benign stranger
come whistling up to the window,
the hobo sun – striking the dust
on the pane, sidling into rooms,
settling, a little bemused, upon a desktop
to finger the small clutter there.
The sun like a stranger in a jaunty hat,
just come back from Away.
Making wondrous the shapes of things.
Giving them shadows.

Doubt is growing, like a shadow in the late afternoon. The shadow of a doubt. Doubt that is its own shadow. Doubt is drawing itself out, a long shadow in the late afternoon, swallowing other shadows. As a cloud shadow swallows other shadows.

To what avail a sundial on a cloudy day?

A longing for times past. For my childhood. For times when my children were children. *May you live to see your children's children.*

(Time like a muscle, flexing. Time and Time's shadows.)

My broken clock – I can no longer count on it to wake me. I will have to buy a new one. But time is money! Can I buy a clock with time I've saved? If I buy a clock, am I buying time? (I am *only* buying time. Till the new clock breaks.)

We live in broken time

## 22

The sound of a thin fiddling drifts to me again from behind the woodshed. (She's back. Long dress blowing against her ankles, lean frame swaying. She's playing variations on yesterday's tune. A call to engage, to pick up my bow – )

Can one take arms against a sea of certainty
with a thin river of doubt? Can one hold out?
Am I a stubborn little river flowing the wrong way
in this world of ours? Against the flow of the times,
against the new certainties –

Doubt was a thread in the gathering dusk. Thin as spider silk. Doubt came winding down from infinite space like a silver thread. Like a thread of river. Like a thread of music. I was following the music, and the music was Doubt. I was following the doubt.

(The cat walks across the page I write on, plumy tail brushing my cheek.)

> *No ideas but in things*
> No answers but in questions

23

Doubt came rolling in like a tide, washing over the writing in the sand. Doubt like a tide, washing in, washing out, effacing old certainties.

"Where is it written? Is it carved in stone?"
– No, it is only traced in sand.

*Yet stones have stood for a thousand years, and pained thoughts found*
*the honey of peace in old poems.*
– That too.

Tatterdemalion man, mankind in rags,
rags of his wisdom, rags of his own undoing

The striving ink, blown dry upon the page

The world held together by rust

World that was.

24

Already the dawn is earlier, the days of the winter-dark
womb-hour are ended.
And Doubt came dancing up with the dawn –

Questions were beginning to sprout
from cracks between the paving-stones.
(Let questions break up the paving-stones.)

Prayers were beginning to push up
from cracks between the paving-stones.
(Let prayers break up the paving-stones.)

Let the roots of great trees heave up the paving-stones
and crack them, let there be
upheaval

(Doubt the Juggler was sending up
silver balls into the air, each one a question.
Keeping them all in motion.)

25

At two hairs past a freckle, I'm reminded that the strap on my watch is broken – the reason my wrist is bare. Pang of annoyance. "A watch is habit-forming," I remark to the friend who walks beside me, and after a pause – the sort of pause that makes you think you have not been heard – he says in his slow-spoken, meditative way, "But so is time."

I am remembering this at a distance of fifty years. I remember his tiny gabled room at the top of an old house on Milton Street, a Spartan room that doubled as painting studio. We were walking back there at night after seeing a movie about Tagore, the Indian poet. We were in company of his friend from India who walked alongside us, a little bit in his own world, humming softly and snapping his fingers to a song of India. Downtown Montreal, early spring, the air mild. Our streetlamp shadows growing and shrinking on the newly bare pavement as we walked.

Of the movie I remember only a woman who came down to the water's edge with bracelets on her ankles – bracelets making music round her ankles. Of the friend, whom I have not seen these forty years, I will soon learn (twenty months after the fact) that he died in a chronic care home, in the first wave of the Virus, "after four years wandering in Alzheimer's labyrinth" according to the eulogy that will come up on screen when, on impulse, I search his name.

26

Our neighbourhood is full of vulnerable souls, frail floaters of an aging generation. (We who lived off the fat of the land. *Born at the right time.*) After winter, the glare of spring sun shows us to each other with a new crop of wrinkles, new gray in our hair, or newly balding. Winter-white and dazed by the light we venture out on our sorties looking like the walking wounded. We are gnomes, we are sticks, our aging cats are bankrupting us, our grown children navigate a world we don't recognize, some of them won't talk to us, our grandchildren live on screens, the littlest calls his father's father *"l'autre grandpère, qui vit dans l'ordinateur"*

Technology is a flytrap. May even have been planned as such. We flew into it unsuspecting, wide-eyed at what man hath wrought, and now we're stuck in the honey, twitching our useless little wings. The honey of convenience. The sap. How it saps us – .

Do we all just bumble through our allotted days, each new stage a different kind of chaos and mismanagement? Every generation bumbling anew, bungling anew? We came in on a tide of peace and prosperity. We will go out into a maelstrom.

(Tatterdemalion man,
we passed you on the street today.
We thought: rags are your riches,
because you have nothing,
nothing to take away.)

27

Someone next door is knocking
on a shared wall, trying to find a beam.
(Neighbour, I hear you.)

Neighbour on the other side,
your kitchen window, sunstruck,
beams reflected sunlight into mine –
sunlight distilled, an eggshell-pale square
that trembles on the floor,
a fleeting visitor, like a rare bird
to the feeder; or like the swift
reflexive smile of a passing stranger
responding to my absent-minded smile.

Weak signals from another realm.
Maybe angels visit every day and I miss them,
mistake them for things of this world?

I'm told some have begun
to call on God again, as an old lover
shies pebbles at a darkened window:
*Do you still live here?*
*Are you awake?*
*Do you remember me?*
It is like someone knocking
on an old plaster wall,
trying to find a beam to sink a nail in.
Something that will hold.

(Grasp that tedious reed,
hope.
        Grasp hope.
That tedious reed.)

## 28

Doubt was at the edge of the wood
in the dusk, twinkling.
Blinking off and on like a firefly.

Doubt was at the junction
at nightfall, signalling.
Flashing on and off like a semaphore.

And the Between –

the Between was a furtive movement in the trackside weeds,
the Between was a rabbit suddenly darting out onto the track,
a rabbit caught in the headlights.

The fugitive Between –
in flight, in hiding,
imperilled.

29

There's a message the dusk brings
to one who sits on outside, alone
as it comes on, and after,
or to one inside, who stands alone
by a window, watching the evening fade,
and does not turn on the light.

The one is alone, and so is the other.
At nightfall, in a world without ballast,
a quiet has descended. The message is wordless.
It is something about where we are, or who we are.
Or both. Something unsayable. Something felt
in the marrow.

Tatterdemalion man, man at the crossing,
poor Tom, Jackself, hobo, madman –
who could not love the wild in you?
Who could not love you for your wildness?

30

O self-appointed, self-anointed
wise ones, sanctioned to chirp
diversity as you smother
otherness of opinion,
you who lend credence to Power
for edicts that hinder our breathing,
muffle our voices, rob us of faces,
board up the little corner stores where we
used to buy taken-for-granted
happiness like penny candy –
see how your absolutes freeze tongues
that might sing in a variant key;
soon you will have stilled the beat
of every different drummer, soon
there will be no rat-a-tat-tat
save your own

*rat-a-tat-tat*
is the tune they're rehearsing
in high places
(dishing up war again! – war!)
and *Save your own*
is what we must say
to our children,
whose children
are in their sights

> *Woe to them who devise iniquity and plot wickedness!*
> *They covet fields and seize them, and houses and snatch them;*
> *they oppress a man and his household,*
> *even a man and his heritage . . .*

> > *save us for thy name's sake; shield us, and remove from us*
> > *the enemy and pestilence, the sword and famine and grief;*
> > *remove the adversary from before us and from behind us*

31

It was the second year of the Virus
it was the year we began saying
"Thank you so much" to each other for
every small kindness or service rendered

Holding our cards closer
to our chests, we grasped
hope (that tedious reed)

Some dismissed hearsay
as hearsay, some
denounced it as heresy

People stoppered their ears against
the "say" they couldn't afford to hear
people said *Let's not go there*

It was all the blind man and the elephant
where the scientists were concerned
and the elephant in the room where
the public was concerned

The man on the street wasn't talking

*spread over us thy shelter of peace, and direct us with good counsel*

*remove from us the enemy and pestilence,*
*the adversary from before us      and behind us*

32

I saw the best minds of my generation
poised to go gentle into
a night to remember, poised
to go not with a bang
but a whimper – or no, not even
a whimper; pledged to go quietly,
branded, muzzled by choice,
all heads bent
to the little screens, all hands
on deck, all sleeves rolled
back for the boost
chanting the new creed
*We're all in this together*
– though we were all in it
very, very separately,
and the dire chorus
of newscasters had already
begun to sing of a new
crisis, latest in the series
of afflictions being visited
upon us for our sins
as a species, viz:        an
"epidemic of loneliness"

something was wrong but
you couldn't name it,
the city after winter
resurrected but dead,
a propped-up corpse, chalky
under the pitiless spring light,
graffiti creeping like a mould
over miles of blanched façades
and shuttered storefronts

I saw the world become
an isotope of itself,
saw human beings on a march
to become human beens,

*brave puppets*
in service to machines

and I was unwilling.
and I was afraid.
(AM. AM. AM. AM. AM.)

*shelter us in the shadow of thy wings*
*for thou art our guarding and saving God*

33

Still –

In a dream I seem to hear them

children's voices in an alley
on a late spring afternoon      the day
gone suddenly cloudy      a wind
out of nowhere raising dust devils
on the cracked cement
children's voices shrilling in an alley
and the sound of running footsteps
(clap of thunder !
                                        gleeful stampede !)
soles of shoes slapping the ground
while a wind out of nowhere
gone suddenly cooler      now bears
unbearable sweetness upward
to the still-open windows
honeysuckle and linden
borne upward with the echo
of children's running footsteps
moments before the rain begins

*shelter us in the shadow of thy wings*

*guard thou our going out and our coming in*
*for life and peace henceforth and forever*

~

## NOTES

Lit Room: The epigraph is from a passage of Talmud quoted in the morning synagogue service, as translated in the *The Complete ArtScroll Siddur* (Hebrew prayer book): "Rabbi Elazar said on behalf of Rabbi Chanina: Torah scholars increase peace in the world, as it is said: 'And all your children will be students of G-d, and your children will have peace' – do not read 'your children' [בָּנָיִךְ] but 'your builders' [בּוֹנַיִךְ.]" Citing Isaiah 54:13, the commentator observes that with the alteration of a single vowel sound, the Hebrew for "your children" can be heard as "your builders."

In Lockdown: *Jusqu'à ce que l'amour nous sépare* translates as "Until love do us part." In French it is a play on words, since *l'amour* (love) and *la mort* (death) are pronounced similarly.

On Reading Hopkins' *No worst, there is none . . .*: from *The Works of Gerard Manley Hopkins*, #41 in Poems 1876–1889 (Wordsworth Editions, 1994).

On Reading Hopkins' *My own heart let me more have pity on . . .* : from *The Works of Gerard Manley Hopkins*, #47 in Poems 1876–1889 (Wordsworth Editions, 1994).

Four Cut Sunflowers, One Upside Down: the last six lines are from a letter Vincent Van Gogh wrote to his brother Theo on December 1, 1883.

1 *Back to the Sea! shouted the brave puppet*: Cartoon caption in *The Berenstain Baby Book*, 1951. The cartoon shows a man and woman waking in bed with a start. In the adjacent moonlit room a toddler, standing in his crib, has managed to switch on a record player on which his Pinocchio record has resumed playing full volume.

3 The italicized last line, from Psalm 4:5, concludes the Hebrew Night Prayer (Philip Birnbaum translation).

10 shoes and ships and sealing-wax: from Lewis Carroll's poem, "The Walrus and the Carpenter."

11 Man doth not live by bread alone: Deuteronomy 8:3
*We're all freeloaders under God*: Spoken by Nanny, the peasant housekeeper in Chekhov's play *Uncle Vanya* (David Mamet translation) as performed in Louis Malle's film *Vanya on 42nd Street.*

12 *From everlasting thou art God* (...): from the hymn "O God our help in ages past."

15 Quotes and references to Genesis 1:1 are based on the King James translation.

16 *Know before Whom you stand*: words frequently engraved in Hebrew above the Ark in synagogues. Ascribed to Rabbi Eliezer (Talmud, Tractate Berakhot).

19 *All the lonely people*: from the chorus of "Eleanor Rigby" (The Beatles).
*When he, whose vocation was Waiting, sat far from home* –: Italicized lines are from "Turning Point" by Rainer Maria Rilke, translated by Stephen Mitchell (Uncollected Poems, 1923–1926, in *The Selected Poetry of Rainer Maria Rilke*, 1980).

20 *The world is so full of a number of things* (...): from Robert Louis Stevenson, *A Child's Garden of Verses*, first published in 1885.

*No ideas but in things* (also in 22): William Carlos Williams, from his book-length poem *Paterson.*

*Work of the eyes is done, now/go and do heart-work*: Rilke, from "Turning Point" (as above).

21 *May you live to see your children's children*: Psalm 128, cited in Hebrew Night Prayer (Birnbaum translation).

23 *Yet stones have stood for a thousand years* ( . . . ): Robinson Jeffers, closing lines of the poem "To the Stonecutters."

26 *Born at the right time*: title of song by Paul Simon.

what man hath wrought: "What hath God wrought!" (from Numbers 23:23) was the first telegraph message sent by Samuel Morse in 1844. On August 17, 1945, in the wake of the atomic bombs dropped on Hiroshima and Nagasaki, an editorial by David Lawrence appeared in *The United States News* (later to become *US News & World Report*) under the headline "What Hath Man Wrought!"

29 Jackself: from the sonnet "My own heart let me more have pity on" by Gerard Manley Hopkins. The poet addresses his soul by this name: "*Soul, self; come, poor Jackself...*"

30–33 *Woe to them who devise iniquity* (...): abridged from Micah 2:1; mixed translations. All other italicized quotes are from the Hebrew Night Prayer (Birnbaum).

## ACKNOWLEDGEMENTS

My thanks to the editors of the following publications in which poems first appeared or have been slated to appear, sometimes in slightly different versions:

*Arc*: "Finders Keepers Losers Weepers," "Flashback (March 21, 2020)," "Found Poem, with Coda"

*Best Canadian Poetry 2020*: "Envoi (Artist's Statement)," originally published in *Juniper*

*Columba*: "Late Journal Entry on a Leap Year's Phantom Day"

*Literary Review of Canada*: "Le Rappel des Oiseaux," "Ballad of the One Year Bride"

*The New Quarterly*: "In the Medical Building Lobby Cafe," "Tapestry," "Shadows in Springtime," "The Last Good Days," "Once More," "On Reading Hopkins' *My own heart let me more have pity on . . .*," "Nothing's Happening Here," "world awaiting war," "Four Cut Sunflowers, One Upside Down," "Invocation"

*Queen's Quarterly*: "Street Hockey on Hutchison and Villeneuve, 1981"

*The Walrus*: "A Festering," "Another Winter"

I am grateful to Marc Plourde and Joan Eichner for their close reading and thoughtful response to evolving drafts of "In the Wilderness."

Once more, my thanks to the dedicated team at Biblioasis, and most especially to Dan and Vanessa for seeing me through completion of this first collection in a decade, and for giving it their blessing.

## ABOUT THE AUTHOR

Poet, writer, literary editor, and musician, Robyn Sarah has lived in Montreal since early childhood. Her writing began to appear in Canadian literary magazines in the 1970s while she completed studies at McGill University and the Conservatoire de musique du Québec. Her tenth poetry collection, *My Shoes Are Killing Me*, won the Governor General's Award in 2015. As well, she has published two collections of short stories, a book of essays on poetry, and a memoir, *Music, Late and Soon* (2021), that interweaves her youth as a professional-track clarinetist with her return at fifty-nine (after a lapse of thirty-five years) to the piano teacher who was her life mentor. From 2010 until 2020 she served as poetry editor for Cormorant Books.